Here, at the end.

Poems by
Alice Teeter

Copyright © 2023 by Alice Teeter
First Edition

All rights reserved under International and Pan-American Copyright Conventions. Except for brief quotations in critical articles or reviews, no part of this book may be reproduced in any manner without written permission from the author.

ISBN 978-1-6653-0614-0

This ISBN is the property of BookLogix for the express purpose of sales and distribution of this title. BookLogix is not responsible for the writing, editing, or design/appearance of this book. The content of this book is the property of the copyright holder only. BookLogix does not hold any ownership of the content of this book and is not liable in any way for the materials contained within. The views and opinions expressed in this book are the property of the Author/Copyright holder, and do not necessarily reflect those of BookLogix.

Cover Art: Elizaveta Karandaeva Copyright © 123RF.COM
No. 7 & 8: pixelpic Copyright © 123RF.COM
No. 32: Sergii Shabanov Copyright © 123RF.COM

Author Photo: Dana Kemp, 2008

Book Design: EMWorld Graphics

Author inquiries and mail orders:
P.O. Box 766
Pine Lake, GA 30072-0766

for my brother David,
who left early to avoid the rush

1.

Here, at the end of the world
things don't taste as good,
but they're easy —
plastic cups contain
insipid coffee and
everybody's doing it —
it saves time.

2.

Will chipmunks still scamper
across empty roadways?
Koalas may not have enough numbers
to survive. The heat index rises.
Swamped and stamped with sizzle,
we begin to float with it.
Here, we are here, we all are
together here in the end —
the lovers — the haters —
who do you say is who?

3.

What will we forget to do
here, at the end —
stir the coffee grounds
so they sink down?

4.

At the end of the world
do we carry our best
luggage empty?

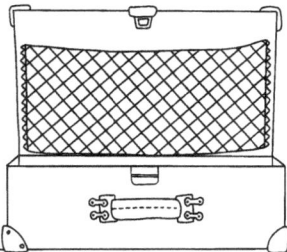

5.

We hope the neighbors
will stop for us.
We've packed the coin collection,
and water, a few clothes,
but we have no way
to get there in the end
unless they come
and pick us up
in their station wagon —
the one with a missing hubcap
and two doors that won't open
and three windows
that won't roll up
or down.

6.

there is still lots of life left
we are yet hopeful —
we poison roaches,
kill ants,
exterminate weeds,
savage spiders,
croak frogs.
Which has more synonyms —
death or life?

7.

Thick boats of magnolia leaves
float on the surface of the pond.
Here, at the end of everything
the fish are shaded —
succored by satisfaction
and the boat tied to the dock drifts
knock   knock   knocking
against the piling
as the planks warp in the sun.

8.

The once-mown field
sprouts young pines —
here, at the end, they spread out
across the rolling meadow —
bright green candles
showing the way.

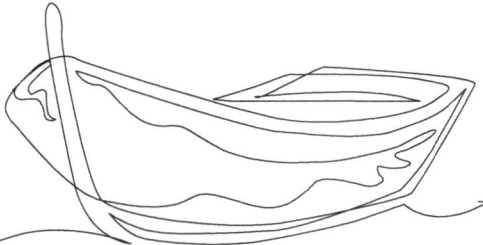

9.

It is so quiet here, at the end —
silence stretches for miles,
a glassy sea becalmed
reflects only blue sky —
the hush complete.

10.

At the end of the world
the barrow cracks open —
the icing seems sweet,
but the cupcakes are dry.

11.

Here, at the end
dust devils whirl.

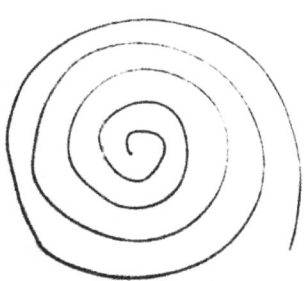

12.

Finally, in the end,
the leaves begin to turn.
One by one they fall,
drift into piles, change
from green to yellow
or orange or red
then brown.
Dry, crumble,
ground to dirt.

13.

Soft rustling sounds in the dry leaves
here, at the end — the scritch scratch
of small furry creatures
searching for bugs and worms
in piles raked up by wind.

14.

A cool breeze finally wafts in
the windows that are all open.
Here, at the end, the fine hairs
on your arms will detect movement
and you will turn your face
into the wind that comes.

15.

When you're fleeing the end of the world,
do you take your long-dead father's clothes
if they are already packed,
suits folded neatly
in a good grip
ready to be zipped closed
and lifted into the car?

16.

Red, blue, and black suitcases,
carry-on size, are stacked
waiting here at the end
for the porter to come,
one leans into another —
they topple over
onto damp dirt and are still.

17.

In the end, a wonderful light —
warm smell of juniper, scent of pine
with every step into the trees.
It's hardly a forest —
a stand, a circle, a block, a strip left
after everything else was bulldozed —
enough to give the illusion that
there are miles of woods on either side.

18.

She forgot the afternoon nap.
Should she take it
on the last day?
Should she sleep
those precious hours away
dreaming?

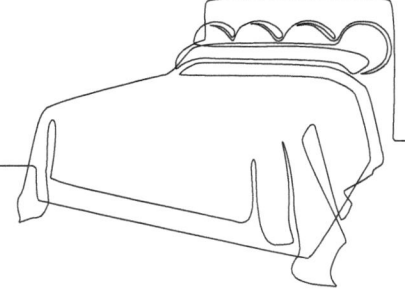

19.

Minutes are ticking
none grabbed saved stopped
sand flows smoothly evenly
grains scatter across the rug —
small dunes build
in the pile carpet
unused
unusable.

20.

Brown-eyed cows sniff the air,
raise their horns,
swing their heads —
here, at the end, they're hungry
for something sweet,
but the apple trees
are in the far pasture
and the gate is closed.

21.

In the end, loud tree frogs
scream in the night,
add their cacophony
to the crickets and cicadas.
Warm moist air blankets
the ground, the sounds are
silvered edges, softened into saucers
to be lapped up, to be spilled
onto long strands of grass
bent by their weight
into arcs over the dirt.

22.

We sit on the rocks in the sun and
hear the sound of one bird calling.
A trill starts each call, a buzz
in the middle of the phrase. We
never hear that last finale –
we leave before the song is done.

23.

Will a wild face peer in the window
at the end — frantic and searching?
Will it be your face —
eyes wide the whites showing
all the way around —
your mouth agape,
your nostrils flared,
your hands spread out
on the windowsill,
ready to jump?

24.

come on come on come on
it's time for the trunks to be packed
it's time for the car to be loaded
it's time to start driving
to the end.

25.

The ducks are still quacking,
even now they mutter
splashing in the wetlands,
riding small rapids
over clumps of greenery
down into the deeper pools,
they don't need to pack for the end
they are always ready.

26.

Here, at the end, an Angus bull,
small and solid red,
bellows mightily, munches
the green grass;
we watch, smell the clods
of earth kicked up
by his hooves;
we are right down here with it
looking up at a blue sky
waiting.

27.

silence complete
no bee buzz
no mosquito choir
no scurry in dry leaves
no birdsong
mention these things
and they sound again
only in a mind
they are no more

28.

It doesn't take long
to fall asleep
after lunch
before the end.

29.

What do we need for the end?
Socks and shoes? Hats?
Will gloves ward off?
Or a coat provide?

30.

At the last, she packs her bags —
the small brown knapsack
a large blue valise
with broken locks.

31.

At the end of the world,
gulls cry.
Foam rolls up across the beach.

32.

The rugs are all red when it comes,
frayed edged flying dusty wrecks;
feet have worn threadbare
tracks through the piles,
a dog has scratched a corner
every night, circling to sleep,
curled nose under paws warm
in the understanding of food.

33.

Sing sing oh sing and dance
step light at the end
a saucepan of milk for the cat
a gentle touch a purr
let the notes soar
the shuffle stomp begin
turn to a prance
pick up your feet
throw your arms wide
welcome it in
what else is there to do?

34.

Packing for the end of the world
requires little thought
just a mad rush of hands
grabbing what's close
and a clatter of shoes
on the wooden floor
in the hall.

35.

Here, at the end of it,
the traveling bags are stacked —
a large pile growing larger as if
waiting for the bell hop
to take them to your room.

36.

when the ocean gets here
we will be washed away
our bodies spreading out
sandcastles
left in the evening tide
dips and ridges evened out.
By morning we will be detritus —
white bone fragments
that litter the beach and are
ground into sharp sand.

37.

The quiet used to be broken
by a leaf blower —
hours spent every day
clearing debris
from the sidewalk,
the yard, the porch.
Now, everything
is slowly worn away
by relentless wind.

38.

Here, at the end, all is consumed —
air earth water fire
used up depleted
the smell of burning tires
kerosene   a taste of ashes
laced with charcoal lighter
the sound of hissing water
rushes through pipes
vents a vibrant whistle.

39.

No ringing bells, no loud hurrahs,
no smell of wood smoke,
no crackle of campfires,
no popping sparks,
no dogs bark.
Here, at the end, all these things
once evoked are gone.

40.

At the end, the shoes by the door,
one turned on its side,
clean of mud and dirt,
waiting for feet to come
slip in, slide on, tie tight,
and tromp tromp tromp away.

41.

Confetti of yellow ginkgo leaves
flutter in the sun and spin,
here at the shattering end,
a mass of maple seeds
whirl on the wind, glitter,
spiral dance in the air —
spreading brilliance everywhere.

42.

Flowers mixed with a pattern —
devoid of anything human —
filigree of lacy shapes.
Are the flowers abomination
here, at the end?
How can they keep blooming
when we are all done?

www.ingramcontent.com/pod-product-compliance
Lightning Source LLC
Chambersburg PA
CBHW081159070526
44583CB00021B/2911